Jack
The Village Cat

DAVID HORRIX

ABOUT THE AUTHOR

David Horrix is the author of several books and holds a First Class Honours Degree and a Masters's (Master of Science) in Psychology. From an early age, David has been deeply interested in the mysteries of existence, the search for meaning, and those individuals who have tried to make sense of human reality.

Incorporated into this series of stories about Jack the Cat are philosophical and psychological themes from some of the world's greatest thinkers, particularly Socrates (469-399 B.C), Epictetus (55-135 C.E), Dostoevsky (1821-1881), May (1909-1994), Frankl (1905-1997) and Van Deurzen (Born 1951).

However, the most significant influence on David's thinking is the writer Antoine de Saint-Exupery (1900-1944), particularly the truths within the classic novella The Little Prince (1943 Le petit prince).

This series of tales about Jack, the cat are exciting stories to read to children or for children to read themselves. However, like The Little Prince (1943 Le petit prince), they have more profound meanings and insights that may be useful to many people of all ages. Towards the end of the book, David explains the philosophy and psychology behind the story about Jack. David hopes you enjoy the stories.

To Prince Ben and Sam, Princess Katie and the Little Princes Erol, Lonnie and Henry, what fun we had, what games we played, and how happy you made me.

Grandpa x

INTRODUCTION

This story is inspired by a remarkable and lovable Tabby cat which just appeared one day sitting on a wall outside a house in a small village in the Yorkshire Dales.

The cat wouldn't leave; seemingly, he had chosen where he wanted to live. The house owner enquired, but it was as if the cat had appeared out of nowhere, so she took him in, called him Jack, cared for him and ensured he got plenty of treats (prawns were his favourite).

It is true that after living comfortably in his new home for several years, Jack decided to leave to live a very different life in the wild on the outskirts of the village near a small school. It is also true that many people grew to love him dearly, miss him dreadfully and still remember him fondly and visit the little wooden bench set amongst the trees, where Jack loved spending time greeting people.

Of course, only Jack can know what really happened when he lived in the wild, and he is no longer around to tell us! However, Jack, the gentlest and most courageous of cats, lived a remarkable life and had many adventures you can read about if you enjoy this one.

"The opposite of courage in our society is not cowardice, its conformity" (Rollo May)

JACK THE VILLAGE CAT

Jack could have lived his life the same way many other domestic tabby cats live theirs. That is to say, comfortably with a friendly owner in a nice home, regular mealtimes, a soft bed to curl up on, and a favourite place to lounge, look out the window and watch the world pass by.

Yes, a regular cat's life could easily have been Jack's lot, living unnoticed because he, like many other cats, did nothing out of the ordinary, nothing peculiar or quirky. Jack was seemingly a quite unremarkable cat!

"But possibly I am something more than I suppose myself to be" (Rene Descartes)

Jack was a little stockier, and his mottled brown fur much thicker than most tabbies, a similar look to that of the wildcats in the North. He had a gentle and calm face, unlike many tomcats who can appear rather angry, always hissing, spitting, and wanting to fight.

Also, Jack liked his own company rather than running around in a gang with the other tomcats; however, he wasn't on bad terms with them but was somewhat indifferent.

Besides his peculiar size and thick fur, Jack appeared like a relatively ordinary cat.

"Hiding under the cat that is, there is a cat that isn't" (Horrix)

Jack's kind owner always ensured that a bowl of cat food and a drink awaited him in her kitchen, so he would never be hungry or thirsty.

Sometimes when Jack ate, he would stop, prick his ears up, and look over his shoulder, sensing that another cat might be near and want to steal his food, similar to how it might be in the wild; of course, there never was.

Jack didn't know what it was like to live without home comforts because this was all he had ever known; seemingly, Jack was a cat that wanted for nothing.

"Without the taste of hunger, abundance brings no pleasure" (Horrix)

Jack would awake quite late in the morning, long after it was light. Somewhat reluctantly, he would leave his warm bed, stretch, shake to awaken himself, wash, and make his way to the kitchen for breakfast.

Jack would then take a morning walk, staying near his home, certainly no more than a street away. Soon Jack returned home and spent the day napping on his bed or watching the world pass by from his window. He walked again in the evenings, staying close to home. He might occasionally hear the hissing and spitting of Tomcats and see the occasional skirmish as they argued over their territory or the affections of the Molly cats.

Still, it was nothing serious, and Jack was never frightened by the Toms, who were wary of his peculiar size. When he returned home, he ate and drank a little before bed. Every day was the same for Jack.

"It's time you realised that you have something in you more powerful and miraculous than the things that affect you and make you dance like a puppet" (Marcus Aurelius)

Some say cats don't think about much; however, Jack was different and thought a lot as he lay on the sill looking out his favourite window. Sometimes raindrops would run down the window pane, or snowflakes fall from the cold grey sky. Sometimes the sun's rays made Jack very drowsy.

But the window sill was a good place where he could think in peace. Jack considered his kind owner, who looked after him and loved him dearly. Jack thought a lot about his life and why although he had every comfort a cat could wish for, he had started to feel restless, as if something was happening somewhere and he wasn't a part of it.

Around this time, when Jack felt fidgety, he began to follow his owner out on her dog walks, often venturing to the outskirts of the village where it was a little wilder.

"Rather than smoothing our path and becoming shadows of what we really are, we should take the rugged hard road and discover our true capabilities " (Van-Deurzen)

One evening, as Jack absent-mindedly looked out of his window after a long day of doing what he usually did, he heard something new yet strangely familiar that made his ears prick up and his heart race with excitement.

Somewhere high in the night sky, a skein of geese flew north, making their strange and haunting honks and cries, trying to stay together on their long, dangerous journey to their breeding grounds. Jack was fascinated by this wild and mysterious sound that made him feel excited but also very restless; something was stirring inside Jack.

"If you do not express your own original ideas, if you do not listen to your own being, you will have betrayed yourself" (Rollo May)

However, Jack soon started to feel that change was in the air; he could almost taste it. Jack's itchy feet made him wander further from his home than before.

He went out earlier in the mornings when his owner was still fast asleep to explore the fields, woods, hedgerows, and places only wild creatures know. Jack often stayed out all day long, only returning home late because he sensed his owner would be terribly concerned about him.

After exploring, Jack was frequently tired and grubby, with burrs stuck to his shabby fur, but he felt less restless and more settled. These days his bowl of food waiting for him in the kitchen was hardly ever touched; Jack was dining elsewhere!

"You must go on adventures to find out where you truly belong"
(Sue Fitzmaurice)

There was one place that Jack liked to visit more than any other, a spot on the outskirts of the village he had discovered when he followed his owner, walking her dog. A narrow lane had on one side a wooden fence in front of a small field with two horses and opposite a stone wall covered in moss with a stream on the far side. A gap in the wall just before an old railway bridge formed the entrance to a narrow path running around the edge of a school.

On one side of the track were trees, plants, and a wooden fence: a large field and a farmhouse in the distance. On the other side of the path was a dense hedgerow with tangled bramble and hawthorn bushes filled with nettles, thistles, and various plants. Set back from the trail was a little wooden bench, a peaceful spot where people could rest and hear the happy sound of children playing in the schoolyard a little distance away and hidden behind the trees. This beautiful place, wild at times, was where Jack loved being the most and made his heart race with excitement because here is where he had many adventures and felt the most at home.

"Many people suffer from the fear of finding oneself alone, and so they don't find themselves at all" (Rollo May)

Spring was a wonderful time for Jack when he would notice the first signs of the warmer weather around him. First, snowdrops, then daffodils and bluebells would make their brief appearance. The swifts, swallows, and cuckoos returned from their overseas holidays, dashing, noisy and argumentative, and the Robins, Thrushes, and Blackbird's dawn chorus sounded in thanks for winter's end. Bumblebees hummed and buzzed, collecting pollen from the flowers, butterflies danced to and fro, and the trees became greener.

The hedgerow flushed with colour, and the animals dashed here and there, full of energy after sleeping through the cold long winter months. Crickets filled the warm fragrant evening air with their chirps, and sometimes there were thunderstorms when the air crackled with lightning flares and rumbled and roared like an angry giant. Jack loved everything about his favourite place, laying in the long cool grass or bathing in the sunlight pools scattered between the shadows of the tree's branches. He felt he belonged here, was a part of nature, and felt its force and pulse. Jack roamed and rested wherever pleased him from early morning until dusk. Still, he always returned to his owner's home reluctantly every night.

"Quick as thought itself, a much-travelled man may recall someplace, and wish `Would I were here, or there`" (Homer)

One late evening, after a long day exploring, a tired Jack stretched out on his usual window sill and looked at the stars in the night sky. His ears suddenly pricked up as he heard the familiar sound of the geese's faint, haunting cries somewhere in the dark.

Soon Jack saw them silhouetted in the moonlight, mysterious and wild, flying in formation, heading north to find new adventures and see different things. At this very moment, Jack realised with every part of his being that he must soon leave his home and its safety to follow his call of the wild; the time was right.

"Decide to be extraordinary and do what you need to do now" (Epictetus c.50-c.120AD)

The following morning Jack did not go out exploring; instead, he waited until his owner was up, always staying near her, brushing against her, and showing her lots of attention. After breakfast, she settled in her comfy chair, and Jack jumped up, curled up in her lap, and rested for many comfortable hours.

Jack remained inside all day and all night, always staying very near his owner, making sure she knew he loved her dearly. The following morning, Jack's bed was empty; he was gone; Jack had made his move!

What bird kept in a cage will not make every effort to escape? I wish to fly where I please, live in the fields, sing as I please
(Epictetus c.50-c.120AD)

Each day Jack's owner would call his name repeatedly, but her appeals went unanswered, even though in the distance Jack could hear her voice faintly, for his favourite place, secret and wild as it was, was not that far from home.

However, for quite some time, he vanished (cats can do that); Jack had gone to ground. There would no longer be the certainty of food and drink, a bed to sleep in, a window to look out of, or a comfy lap to curl up on.

Jack needed all of his courage; however, he was excited for whatever challenges life had in store for him.
Jack was ready!

"Wherever you go, go with all your heart"
(Confucius)

Jack's favourite place became his new home, the place he loved more than any other and where he felt like the genuine Jack! Few people walked along the little path around the school; however, people sometimes took their dogs that way for their walks.

On nice days, teachers from the nearby school took the children to learn about wildlife, plants, and trees. People occasionally would notice a rather large and gentle-looking cat lying in the long grass, sitting in a sunny spot, or resting under the little wooden bench slightly away from the path.

The children loved it when they caught sight of the cat, and Jack loved seeing and hearing the schoolchildren and would often go to greet them and allow them to fuss over him. Jack was remarkably patient and gentle with the children.

"Two roads diverged in a wood, and I took the one less travelled" (Robert Frost)

Occasionally, dogs that didn't know Jack's nature would try to frighten him by running up and barking loudly. However, Jack didn't scare easily; he wouldn't run away; he stood his ground, and if any dog, big or small, got too close, Jack would give it a tap on its nose with his paw to warn it off, usually, all that was required was a warning.

He didn't want to fight, being gentle by nature, but Jack was more than capable of looking after himself if he had to. However, when dogs or other animals understood how brave he was, they soon backed away, crying, whimpering, and didn't dare trouble him again on their walks. Jack was gentle but also firm when he needed to be!

"Blessed god, give me the courage to stand my ground within the laws of peace – shunning hostility and hatred and the fate of violent death" (Homeric Hymn 17)

Word soon spread around the village that a friendly tabby cat lived wild amongst the trees and hedgerows alongside the little path near the school. Jack's owner heard these stories and realised it could be her Jack. She was so excited to think he might not be too far away.

She walked down the little path to the wooden bench where she had heard the wild cat liked to go and sat down to wait and hope. And in no time at all, who should appear? Jack, who came running, jumped up on the bench, purred with happiness and rubbed against his dearest owner.

Both were overjoyed to see each other. Jack's owner spent quite some time with Jack, who laid in her lap as she gently stroked him, but when it was home time, she did not try to take him back because she understood how he needed to live now; so, she let him be. However, it comforted her to know Jack was living quite close. What joy for both of them!

"One's life has value so long as one attributes value to the life of others, by means of love, friendship, indignation and compassion" (Simone de Beauvoir)

So it was, for many years, that Jack lived a wild and free existence, a gypsy cat sleeping in the dense hedgerow, empty fox burrows or in the hollow of trees to shelter from the rain.

Stealthily, silently In the rising mists of dawn and the twilight of dusk, Jack would hunt for food, find drink from a stream, and then sleep throughout the day, resting in the sunlight streaming through the tree branches or sheltering from the wind and rain in the dense and warm hedgerow.

Jack, a Supertramp of a cat, had found true joy in his life by living in his favourite place, wild, free, and happy; Jack had become Jack!

"You must be ready to burn yourself in your own flame; how could you rise anew if you have not first become ashes?"
(Friedrich Nietzsche)

However, there were dangers, and Jack needed to be careful because the owls, hawks, and foxes were always there, viewing him as a tasty meal. Yet Jack was by no means easy prey; his stocky frame and shabby dense fur made him look intimidating and wild, and he had the heart of a lion.

He was usually left well alone by the other creatures who knew that Jack could protect himself even from the foxes who seemed interested in his every move. However, Jack understood because he realised they were just hungry like him and had families to feed. In Jack's new home, dangers were everywhere, and Jack knew he must stay alert to survive. Jack's life was, at times, a precarious existence.

"I don't hate the foxes; they are not cruel like people can be, they just have needs, and it just so happens that one of their needs is me" (Jack Cat)

In wintertime, food became harder to find; Jack knew the feeling of hunger, but he didn't let it concern him unduly because he wasn't helpless; he was strong and capable; after all, Jack was a hunter, and his owner would never let him starve.

The days could be harsh with biting cold wind, sleety painful rain, ice, and deep snow, but Jack's dense fur grew even thicker in the wintertime, and he could look out from his secret grass-lined hiding places in some comfort, enjoying the few hours of daylight. Jack knew winter would not last forever; he could wait it out.

"He who has found a why to live for can bear almost any how" (Nietzsche)

Summers are kinder, a time of plenty for the animals when food is abundant. However, Jack wasn't greedy and only took what he needed to survive, to take the edge off his hunger and quench his thirst, nothing more. Jack's wild-caught food tasted good, and the stream water was sweet and refreshing.

On hot summer nights, Jack might lay under a blanket of twinkling stars watching the yellow harvest moon floating above so close he felt he could touch it with his paw; in the daytime, laze contentedly in the sun when and wherever he pleased. Summers's peace and tranquillity built Jack's strength for the hard winter ahead. Still, he occasionally had to fight to protect himself from the other animals, particularly farm cats who wanted his territory for themselves. These farm cats could be spiteful and dangerous, and Jack sometimes needed all his strength and courage to protect his home from them.

"Just as snow-bearing wintry storms give way to fruitful summer, the everlasting circle of the night gives way to blazing daylight; fearful winds subside and lull to rest the groaning sea; even all-powerful sleep loosens its shackles" (Sophocles c.496-406BC)

Sometimes, perhaps once or twice a year, Jack would be visited by a Molly cat, who was curious about how he lived, which seemed more interesting and exciting than the tomcats she knew; he was different. Jack was always pleased to see her, and they enjoyed doing simple things together, lazing in the mid-morning sun or finding shade from the afternoon's heat in a secret place where they would not be disturbed.

Molly cat was less wild by nature than Jack, and when twilight darkened, she nervously returned to the safety of her home. Jack understood that his life was hard, dangerous, and not for everyone, so he never tried to persuade her to stay however much he wanted to.

"My Molly, I will wait for thee forever, my Dulcinea del Toboso, I am your Knight errant, your noble Jack of hearts, forever bound to you by chivalrous deed and courtly love" (Jack)

Jack's owner often sat with him on the wooden bench set back from the little path, surrounded by trees and sweet-smelling wildflowers, their special place to be together. Jack would enjoy resting on his owner's lap, briefly remembering the comforts of his past life as a domestic cat. Jack's owner would often bring little treats, particularly the prawns he loved to eat when he lived in his owner's house; however, the wild food he hunted tasted better now.

Many other people became aware of Jack and would purposely walk along the little path to see him finding something curious about how he was living. Jack enjoyed greeting people, provided they were kind and didn't throw sticks and stones at him (as some boys did). Jack was well known to the people of the nearby village, so company was never far away if he needed a little companionship which all cats do at times.

"People have forgotten this truth," the fox said. "But you mustn't forget it. You become responsible forever for what you've tamed" (Antoine de Saint-Exupery)

The small school near where Jack lived was a special place for Jack. Each day he could hear the comforting sound of children in the nearby school playground, the bell when playtime was over, and the excited chatter when parents picked their children up from school. The teachers had grown used to Jack being around and became very fond of him, and of course, the children loved Jack.

On one occasion, a school teacher called Jane, who loved Jack dearly, took him to the school assembly, where the children squealed with delight that the cat from the woods had come to visit them. Jack loved seeing and hearing the schoolchildren as they fussed over him. Each bonfire night (November 5th), the school held a fireworks display, and Jack always found a nice spot on a wall or a patch of ground where he could watch the event. He wasn't in the least bit frightened by the noise — Jack was a fearless cat.

"A gentle teacher who shows kindness and love lives forever in the children's hearts" (Horrix)

People found Jack intriguing and still do. Perhaps it was the courage he showed when he questioned if living the way most cats live was right for him. Jack chose a different way and completely changed his life. He found the meaning that had been lacking and stopped feeling restless. Jack then faced many new experiences and challenges.

Through these, he grew from a somewhat ordinary Tabby cat into something extraordinary, more courageous, someone even Jack didn't know existed. Very few cats do what Jack did, preferring the safety and comforts of a home; however, that was much too high a price for a cat like Jack to pay for his freedom. Some people described Jack as half-wild and half-domestic because he was friendly and lived outdoors. In truth, Jack was nearly all wild but loved the company of those who showed him kindness.

Jack was unique and, by nature, gentle, strong, brave, and wild. He had a wonderful life filled with marvellous adventures; you can read the other stories about Jack's life.
Jack left his mark!

25/08/2022 It was only today that I decided to visit where Jack used to live; who should I bump into but Jack's owner? She told me many stories about Jack, and it was clear that she still missed him terribly.

She also said to me that several people walking along the little path around the school grounds swear they still catch glimpses of Jack in and amongst the bushes and the undergrowth.

Perhaps this is wishful thinking, but it wouldn't surprise me because it still feels like he is there when I visit his sacred grove. Take a look, and you will feel what I mean.

"Whosoever is delighted in solitude is either a wild beast or a God" (Aristotle)

The End

JACK THE CAT THAT HELPED HIMSELF (HIS PHILOSOPHY AND PSYCHOLOGY)

"The secret of man's being is not only to live but have something to live for." (Dostoevsky,1981)

According to Socrates (469-399 B.C), "an uninvestigated life is not worth living." (Cooper and Hutchinson 1997, p.33). Socratics "encourage rigorous personal examination and improved knowledge of self as the only meaningful pathway to personal happiness" (Corlett,1996). This approach requires the individual to ask tough questions to obtain knowledge of what "real" goods are, i.e., knowledge and virtue and "illusory" goods, i.e., celebrity, wealth, beauty etc (Kreeft, 2014). This knowledge "cannot be received from others"; it must come from the individual (Corlett,1996).

Jack began to spend a great deal of time thinking and examining his life, and despite having a very comfortable existence, he began to feel restless. Frankl (1952), in Mans Search For Meaning, describes an "Existential Vacuum" where despite the increased wealth that people enjoy, many individuals are plagued by "inner emptiness" and a lack of worthwhile meaning in their lives.

Dostoevsky (1981) wrote that even with "bread in abundance", man would "rather destroy himself than remain on earth" in a life without meaning and faith. As Jack got to "know himself", he realised that his dependence on "illusory goods" (a nice home, bed, food etc.) was harming his true self, and his life lacked meaning.

"What saves a man is to take a step. Then another step. It is always the same step, but you have to take it" (Saint-Exupéry, 1939)

When Jack first heard the geese flying North, it made him anxious and restless. However, according to May (1953, p.27), "anxiety is nature's way of indicating to us that we need to solve a problem." Jack began to explore, going further from his home than before. "Rather than smoothing our path and becoming shadows of what we really are, we should take the rugged hard road and discover our true capabilities" (Van Deurzen, 2010, p.15). When Jack returned home after exploring, he felt "less restless, more settled". Eventually, he discovered a place where he " loved being the most and made his heart race with excitement".

"The important thing is to strive towards a goal which is not immediately visible. That goal is not the concern of the mind, but of the spirit" (Saint-Exupéry, 1942)

In the book Wind, Sand and Stars Saint-Exupéry (1939) suggests that man holds within a mysterious latent passion; circumstances can produce a "curious transformation" where they may discover "a mysterious creature" born of themselves. Finding this "strange tide" and call of duty overrides the domestic security of everyday existence and the need to accumulate material "treasures". In these circumstances, Saint-Exupery suggests that man releases the "sheltered prince" from within. When Jack heard the geese flying north for the second time, he "realised with every part of his being that he, too, must soon leave his home and its safety to follow his call of the wild"; the time was right for Jack to release his "sheltered prince".

"Life ultimately means taking the responsibility to find the right answer to its problems and to fulfil the tasks which it constantly sets for each individual" (Frankl, 1952).

The stoic philosopher Epictetus (55-135 C.E) believed that individuals are not just "passive victims of disturbing emotions" (Long 2013 p250). Frankl (1952) believed that each individual's mission in life demands fulfilment, and the primary motivational force is the striving to find "meaning" in a person's existence. "What human beings can be, they must be" (Maslow and Frager, 1954).

Jack knew what he wanted to do with his life and how he wanted to live (in his favourite place); he found the meaning that had been missing and had made him so anxious. However, before Jack left to start his new life, he wished to show his owner how much he loved her because "you become responsible forever for what you have tamed" (Saint-Exupery,1943).

"The sea is not less beautiful in our eyes because we know that sometimes ships are wrecked by it" (Weil,1951)

Jack left his home and the certainty of food, drink, and a cosy bed. However, according to Jaspers (1883-1969), "it is uncertainty and suffering that brings us to life". Van Deurzen (2010, p.15) suggests, "What one should aspire to is not the easy, effortless happy life, but the work of the living, the labour of life with all its challenges and difficulties". Jack's new home was beautiful, but he needed to be careful; there were dangers "because the owls, hawks, and foxes were always there, viewing him as a tasty meal." However, Jack was brave and "Those who have a why to live can bear with almost any how"(Friedrich Nietzsche)

"You must be ready to burn yourself in your own flame; how could you rise anew if you have not first become ashes?"(Nietzsche, 1883)

Karl Jaspers (1883-1969) suggests that modern society has evolved into a state of 'mass standardisation' where the individual and their uniqueness become lost, and existential philosophy represents the struggle for individuals to resist this tendency and lead a truly authentic existence.

Therefore, existentialist philosophers' concern is for 'freedom' and the individuals' ability to exercise this by taking the 'decisions' and 'responsibility' to determine and shape their future, distinguish themselves as unique individuals and become 'authentic' to themselves (Cogswell and Lee, 2008). Jack exercised his freedom and took responsibility for making the decisions that would change his life and give it meaning (he burnt himself in his own flame).

Dostoevsky (1981, p.306) wrote that individuals have "no more pressing, agonising need than to find someone to whom he can hand over as quickly as possible the gift of freedom with which the poor wretch comes into the world (make us your slaves but feed us)". Jack reached a point where he could no longer be a slave to security and could no longer hand over his freedom, even if this meant facing hardships.

Dostoevsky believed that suffering was an essential and unavoidable aspect of living and a necessary part of man's psychological and spiritual development "Only through suffering can we find ourselves" (Dostoevsky).

Dostoevsky's existential perspective is that man cannot find happiness by avoiding suffering; instead, happiness may ensue by facing suffering with courage "To love is to suffer, and there can be no love otherwise" (Dostoevsky).

Jack transformed his life of dependency and felt much less anxious, distinguished himself as a unique cat, and became 'authentic' to himself. From the existential perspective, not facing with courage the "big questions" and abdicating our existential responsibility to make choices can, according to Nesti (2006), result in despair, a "loss of self", and a "profound imbalance in our mental outlook".

"Humans rarely credit cats with having much sense — cats are unlikely to credit most humans with having any" (Horrix).

Jack was a remarkable cat. I only had the joy of meeting him on two occasions towards the end of his life, but he did have something magical about him.

REFERENCES

Cogswell, D. and Lee, J., 2008. Existentialism For Beginners. Newburyport: For Beginners, p.75.

Cooper, J.M. and Hutchinson, D.S. eds., 1997. Plato: complete works. Hackett Publishing.

Corlett, J., 1996. Sophistry, Socrates, and sport psychology. The Sport Psychologist, 10(1), pp.84-94.

Dostoevsky, F., 1981. The Brothers Karamazov.

Dostoyevsky, F. and Garnett, C., 1981. The brothers Karamazov. p.306.

Frankl, V., 1992. Man's search for meaning. penguin.

Kreeft, P., 2014. Socrates' Children: Ancient: The 100 Greatest Philosophers.

May, R., 1953. Man's search for himself. Norton, p.27.

Long, A., 2013. Epictetus. clarendon press, p.250.

Maslow, A. and Frager, R., 1954. Motivation and personality. New Delhi: Pearson Education.

Nesti, M., 2006. Existential psychology and sport. London: Routledge.

Nietzsche, F. 1883. Thus Spoke Zarathustra.

Saint-Exupéry, A., 1939. Wind, sand and stars.

Saint-Exupéry, A., 1942. Flight to Arras. New York: Harcourt, Brace & World.

Saint-Exupery, A., 1943. Le Petit Prince.

Van Deurzen, E., 2010. Everyday mysteries. London: Routledge, p.15.

Weil, S., 1951. Waiting for God. London: Routledge & K. Pau

FINALLY, THE REAL JACK

CARDS FROM THE SCHOOLCHILDREN

JACK AND HIS LOVING AND FAITHFUL
OWNER LYNEE

"People have forgotten this truth," the fox said. "But you mustn't forget it. You become responsible forever for what you've tamed" (Antoine de Saint-Exupery)

Printed in Great Britain
by Amazon

21989566R00023